This book belongs to:

....

First published in 2014 by Alison Green Books
An imprint of Scholastic Children's Books
Euston House, 24 Eversholt Street
London NW1 1DB
A division of Scholastic Ltd
www.scholastic.co.uk
London – New York – Toronto – Sydney – Auckland
Mexico City – New Delhi – Hong Kong

Based on *Tiddler*, the original picture book
by Julia Donaldson and Axel Scheffler

ISBN: 978 1 407142 85 2

The Tiddler Activity Book

By Julia Donaldson

Illustrated by Axel Scheffler

ALISON GREEN BOOKS

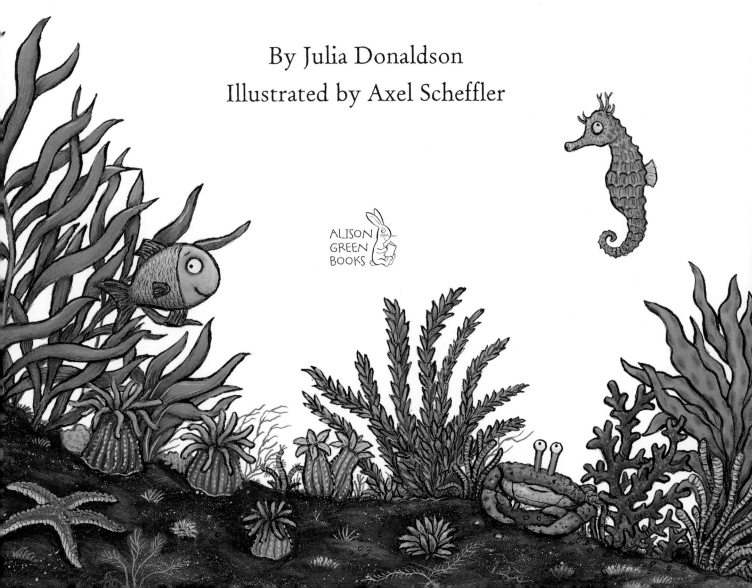

Good Morning, Class!

Who is calling the register? Join the dots to find out.

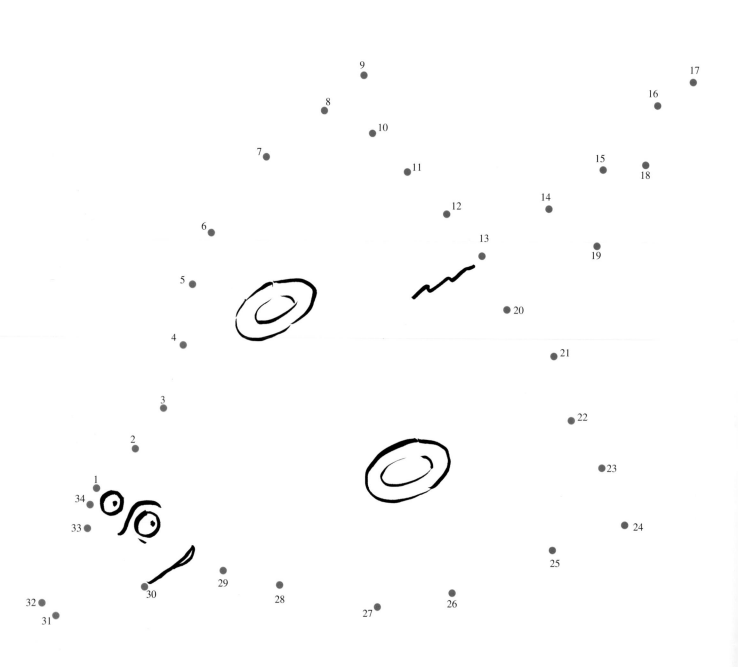

Where is Granny Dory?

Which line will lead Johnny Dory to his granny?

A.
B.
C.
D.
E.
F.
G.

Granny Dory

Draw an Underwater Scene

Can you add to this watery scene?
You could draw a fish, a dolphin, or even Tiddler!

The Fishermen

There are four pieces missing from this jigsaw. They're all in the sticker section at the back of the book. Find them and complete the jigsaw.

Snap! Snap!

Who rescues Tiddler from a squid? Join the dots to find out.

Papier-Mâché Fish

You will need:

PVA glue
1 balloon
Newspaper
Plastic cup
Stiff white card
Scissors
Safety pin
Paintbrushes
Large re-sealable container
Different-coloured paints
Felt pens

As each layer can take a long time to dry, this would be a great project to make over a half-term holiday, spending half an hour on your fish each day. If you have less time, take a look at the shorter version over the page.

To make the fish's body:

Day 1

1. Mix together one cup of glue with half a cup of water in a large, re-sealable container. Tear the newspaper into long strips.
2. Blow up the balloon and tie the end. Stand the balloon in a plastic cup so you can reach all around it.
3. Now stick on your first layer of newspaper. Take one strip at a time and stick it on to the balloon by painting over it with the glue mixture. When your balloon is completely covered, leave it to dry.

Day 2

When the first layer is thoroughly dry, add another layer of newspaper in the same way and leave to dry again.

Don't forget to seal the glue container so your mixture is ready to use tomorrow!

Day 3
Add a final layer of newspaper.

Day 4
When everything is dry, take a safety pin, pop the balloon and pull it out.
You can now decorate your fish!

Decorating your fish:

1. Paint your fish's body.
2. Make fins and a tail by cutting out shapes from the white card – you will need to leave an extra tab along one side to attach them to the fish's body.
3. Paint the fins and tail and glue them on to the fish's body.
4. Cut out two circles of card for eyes and draw black dots on them for pupils. Stick the eyes on – and your fish is finished!

Always ask a grown-up to help when you're using scissors

Make a Tiddler!
(Quick option)

1. Blow the balloon up to the size of a grapefruit.
   Make up the glue mixture as on the previous page.
2. Use coloured tissue paper torn into strips. Paste about
   four layers of tissue on to the balloon without waiting
   for each layer to dry, making sure there are no gaps.
3. When the balloon is covered in tissue paper,
   leave it to dry out.
4. Once dry, pop the balloon and pull it out of the
   papier-mâché shell.
5. You can decorate your fish by drawing on him with a
   black marker and adding fins as shown on the previous page.
6. Colour the fins with different-coloured marker pens.

Top Tip:
Why don't you
try adding glitter
for a sparkly
fish!

Make Your Own Tiddler Bunting

You will need: scissors, glue,
1.5m string, ribbon or cotton

1. Cut around all the coloured triangles.
2. Fold along all the dotted lines.
3. Take one triangle. Carefully glue along
   the tab at the top, then fold it over
   the string or ribbon, starting
   15cm from the end.
4. Repeat with all the triangles
   until you have a lovely string
   of bunting to hang in
   your room!
   (See picture overleaf.)

Always ask
a grown-up to
help when you're
using scissors

glue along
these tabs

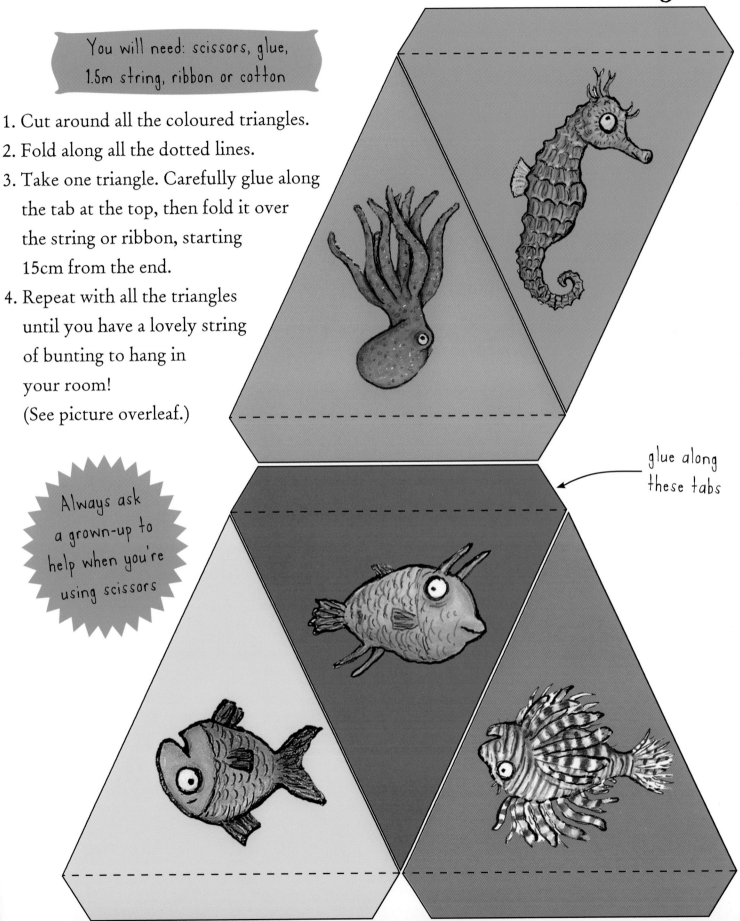

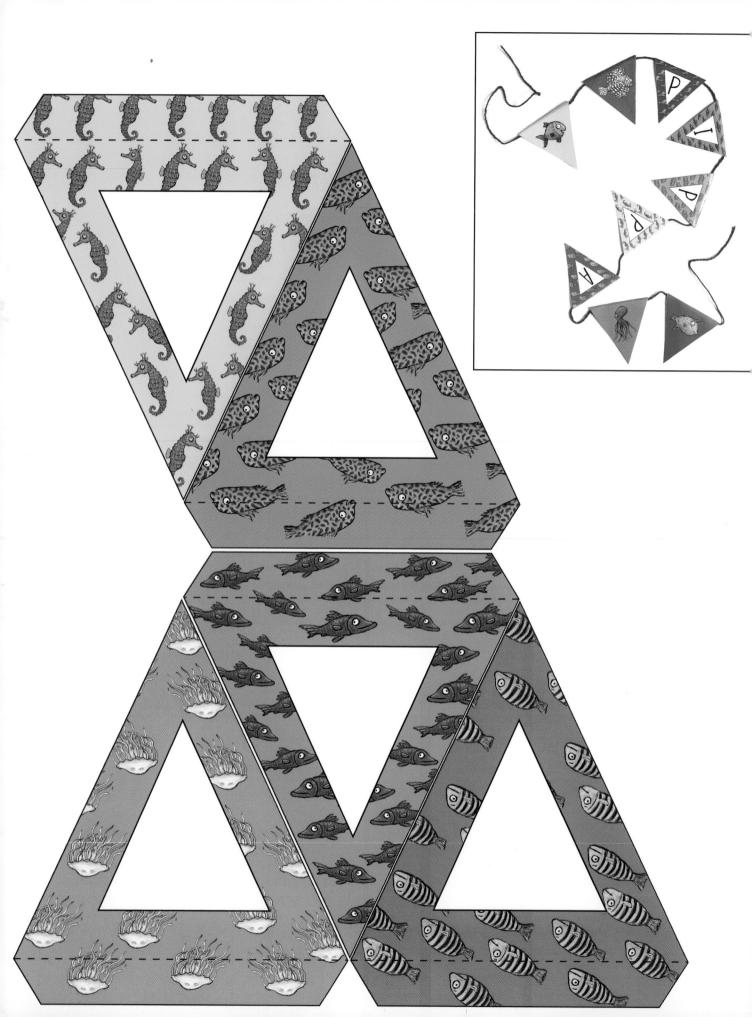

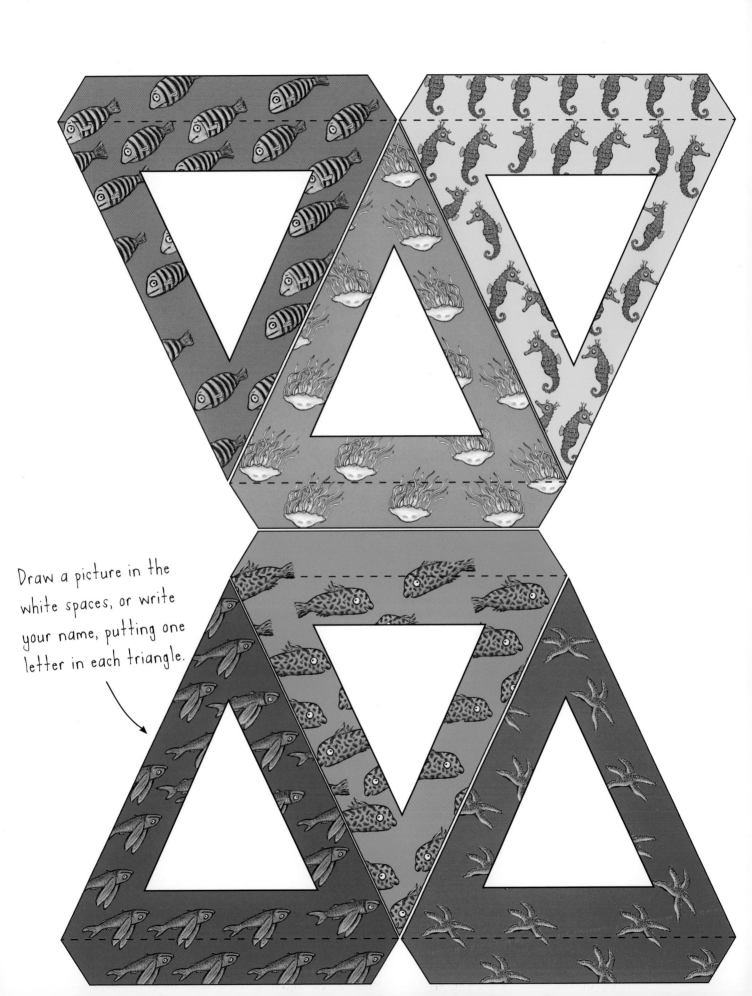

Draw a picture in the white spaces, or write your name, putting one letter in each triangle.

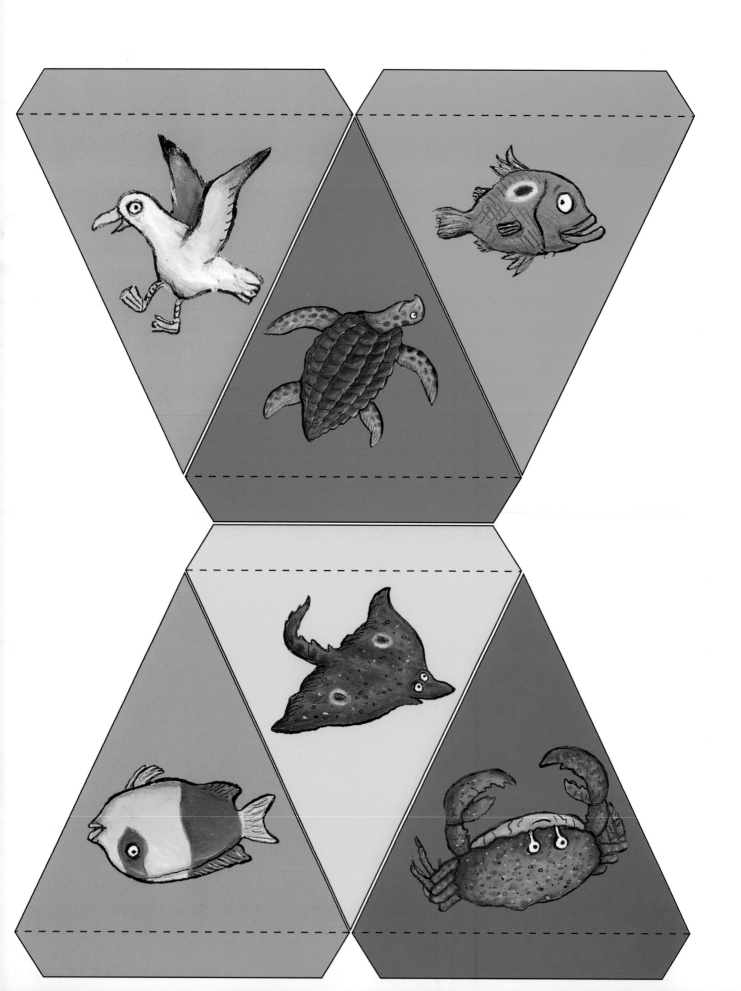

Tiddler's Lost!

Can you help Tiddler find his writer friend?

Clickety-clack!

Who's this scuttling along the sea floor?
Join the dots to solve the mystery.

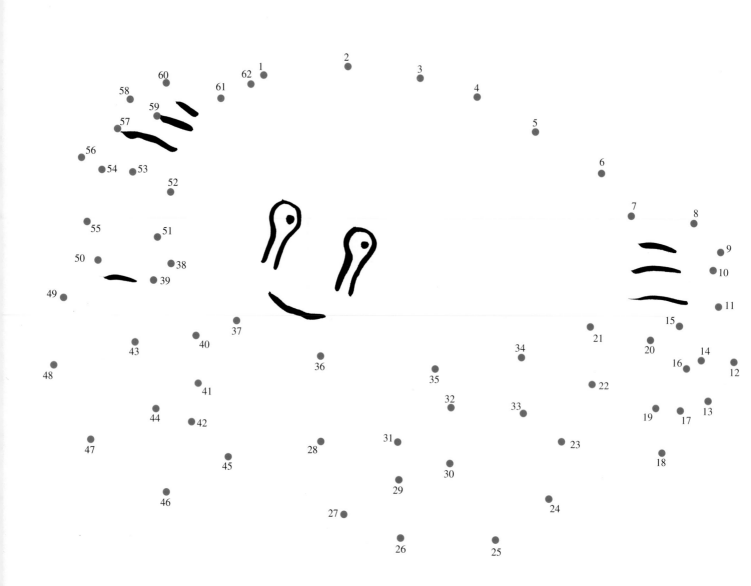

Swimming Round a Shipwreck

Can you colour in this picture?

Fish School

Can you help the fish
with their lessons?

Can you count the jellyfish?

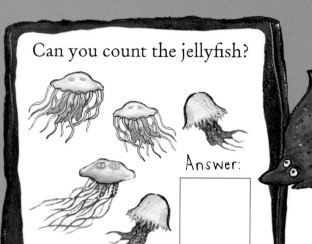

Answer:

Can you do the sums?

$1 + 2 =$

$2 \times 2 =$

Which fish is the odd one out?

Can you match the pairs?

Can you match the colours to the fish?

Grey

Red

Yellow

Green

Blue

Can you trace Tiddler's name?

Tiddler

Can you write your own name?

....

....

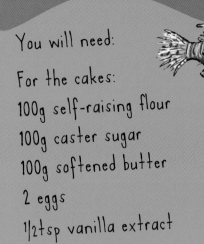

You will need:

For the cakes:
100g self-raising flour
100g caster sugar
100g softened butter
2 eggs
1/2tsp vanilla extract

For the decoration:
50g softened butter
125g icing sugar (sifted)
1 tbsp milk
Food Colouring
Brightly coloured sweets
Strawberry laces (optional)

Mixing bowl
Whisk (hand or electric)
Cupcake cases
Muffin tin
Wire rack
Sieve

Rainbow Fish Cupcakes

Make your very own shimmering shoal with this simple recipe!

To make your cakes:

Preheat the oven to 180°C/380°F/Gas 4.

1. In a large bowl, whisk the sugar and butter together till they're light and fluffy.
2. Break the eggs into the bowl and add the vanilla extract.
3. Sift in the flour, and mix together.
4. Place the cupcake cases in a muffin tin and fill each one about two-thirds full.
5. Cook for 10-15 minutes. They will turn a golden-brown when ready.
6. Place the cupcakes on a wire rack and leave to cool.

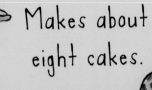

Makes about eight cakes.

To decorate your cakes:

1. In a bowl, add the milk to the softened butter. Gradually sift in the icing sugar and beat it all together until the mixture is light and fluffy.
2. Pour a few drops of food colouring into the mixture, and stir.
3. Smooth the icing on to each cupcake.
4. Use the brightly coloured sweets and strawberry laces to give your fish eyes, lips and scales. You can use a little dot of melted chocolate or chocolate spread to give the eyes pupils.

Always ask a grown-up to help you when you're cooking

Match the Shadow

Can you match the shadows to the right pictures?

Squawk! Squawk!

Who could this be? Find out by joining the dots.

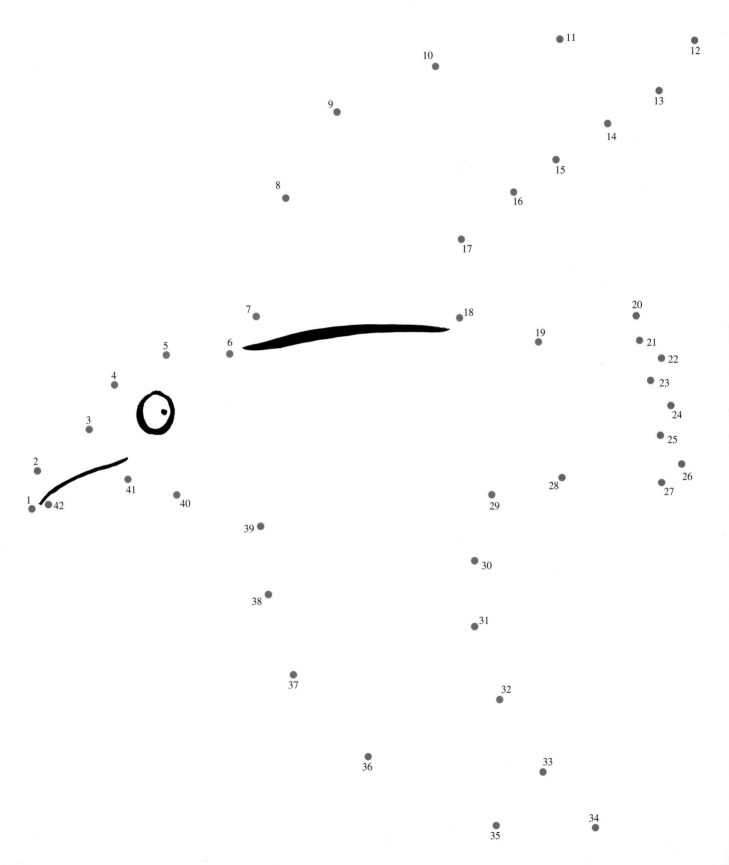

Spot the Difference

There are five differences between these two pictures.

Can you spot them all?

Answers: The mermaid's tail has changed colour from blue to red and a starfish has appeared in her hair. The pufferfish has turned away from the shark. The orange fish has disappeared from the ocean floor and a fish has appeared above the mermaid's tail.

Lunchtime

Can you colour this picture of
the fish eating their lunch?

Turtle Time!

Make your own terrific turtle!

Always ask a grown-up to help when you're using scissors

You will need:

2 paper bowls
White card or craft foam
White paper
Different-coloured paints
PVA glue
Scissors
Pencil
Black marker
Tracing paper
Paper clips
Paint brushes
Sticky tape

To make your turtle shell:

1. Paint the outside of two paper bowls. One will be for the top of the turtle's shell and the other for his belly.
2. Decorate the top of the shell with different-coloured splodges and designs and let both bowls dry.

To complete the turtle:

1. Trace the shape of the flippers, head and tail opposite with tracing paper. Don't forget to trace two of each flipper! Stick the traced shapes on to some card with tape.

2. Carefully cut around both at once.
3. Paint the flippers, head and tail - they could match your turtle's body or be a completely different colour.

FRONT
FLIPPER
(You will need two of these)

HEAD

BACK
FLIPPER
(You will need
two of these)

TAIL

These are the
templates for you
to trace

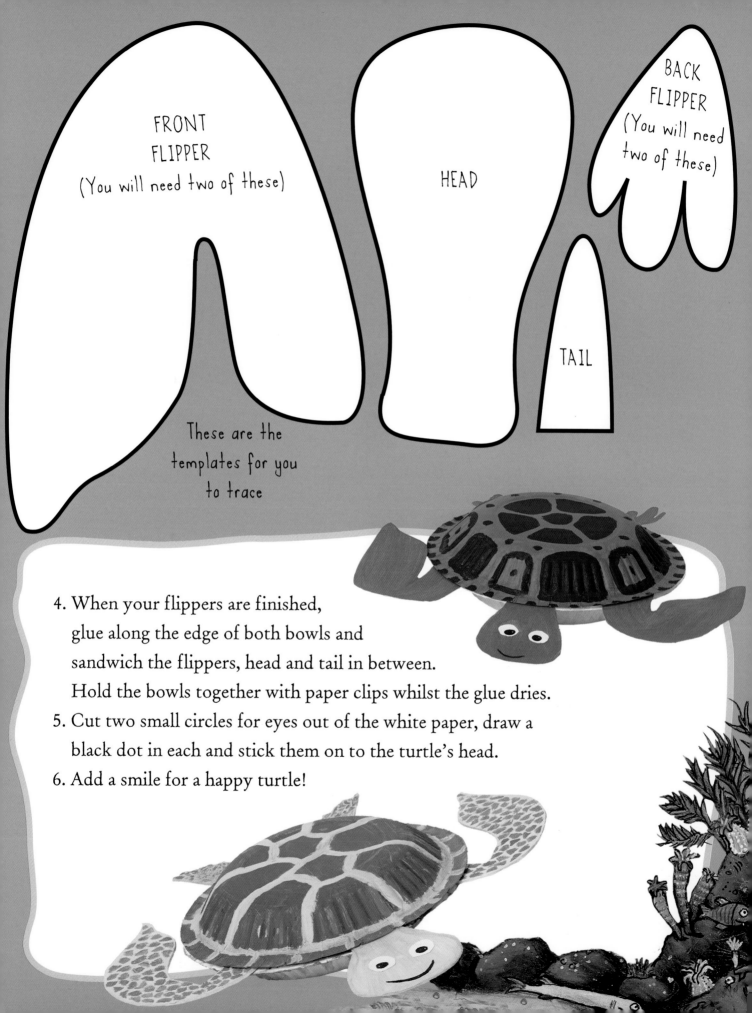

4. When your flippers are finished,
   glue along the edge of both bowls and
   sandwich the flippers, head and tail in between.
   Hold the bowls together with paper clips whilst the glue dries.
5. Cut two small circles for eyes out of the white paper, draw a
   black dot in each and stick them on to the turtle's head.
6. Add a smile for a happy turtle!

Shipwreck

There are four pieces missing from this jigsaw.
They're all in the sticker section at the back of the book.
Can you find them and complete the scene?

Colour Word Search

There are five colours hidden in this word search. One has already been circled for you - can you find the other four?

BLUE
(already circled)

PINK

Y	F	P	G	B	A
E	D	I	R	L	B
L	E	Y	E	S	L
L	O	K	E	R	U
O	R	A	N	G	E
W	T	P	I	N	K

YELLOW

ORANGE

GREEN

Spot the Difference

There are five differences between these two scenes. Can you spot them all?

Yes, Miss Skate!

Miss Skate is calling the register.

Can you colour the scene?

A Fish With a Big Imagination

Who can this be? Join the dots to solve the mystery.

Cheesy Starfish Biscuits

Tiddler loves nibbling on these delicious snacks. Why don't you make some to share?

Preheat the oven to 170°C/325°F/Gas 3.

1. Combine all of the ingredients in a large bowl and knead with your hands until you have a soft dough. (You can also make this by whizzing all the ingredients together in a food processor.)

2. Shape the dough into a disc, wrap it in clingfilm and leave it to rest in the fridge for 15 minutes.

3. Roll out the dough with a rolling pin on a floury surface until it's as thick as a pound coin. Cut out your starfish with the cutters. You can keep re-rolling this dough and cutting out starfish until it is all used up.

4. Place the starfish on the lined baking tray and bake in the oven for about 10 minutes, till golden.

5. Put the starfish on a wire rack – they'll crisp up a bit more as they cool.

You will need:

100g finely grated Red Leicester or Cheddar cheese
25g softened butter
50g plain flour
¼ teaspoon baking powder
Clingfilm
Large bowl
Rolling pin
Star-shaped cookie cutter
Wire rack
Baking tray lined with baking parchment

The Middle of the Ocean

Can you colour in this picture of the strange fish Tiddler meets?

Finger Puppets

Act out your own Tiddler stories with these finger puppets.

cut along the dotted lines

Always ask a grown-up to help when you're using scissors

Wrap these tabs around your finger and fasten with sticky tape.

I heard it from a . . .

There are five words hidden in this wordsearch. We've found one to get you started - can you find the other four?

PLAICE
(already circled)

EEL

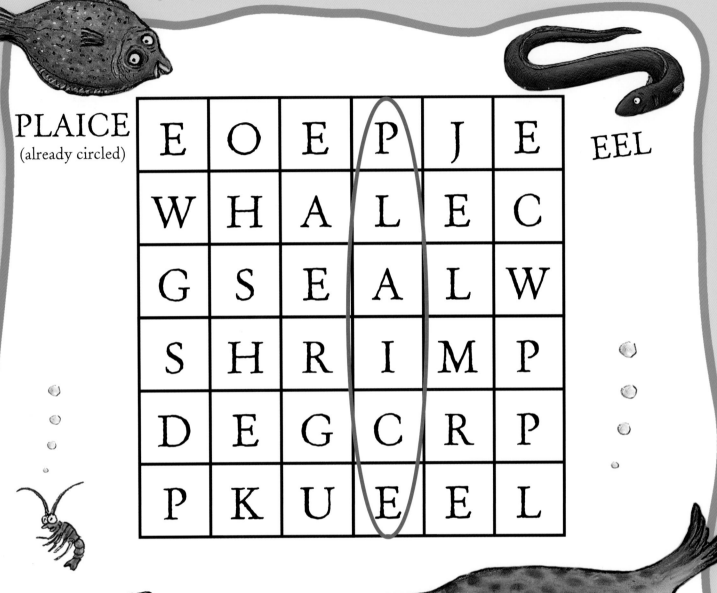

E	O	E	P	J	E
W	H	A	L	E	C
G	S	E	A	L	W
S	H	R	I	M	P
D	E	G	C	R	P
P	K	U	E	E	L

SHRIMP

SEAL

WHALE

You will need:

2 large egg whites
100g caster sugar
250g shredded coconut
1 teaspoon vanilla extract
1 pinch of salt
50g milk chocolate
Hundreds and thousands
Large bowl
Small bowl
Baking sheet lined with
   baking parchment
Whisk (hand or electric)
Ice-cream scoop
Wire rack
Heatproof bowl

Sea Urchin Macaroons

These tasty teatime treats
look like sea urchins!

Always ask a grown-up to help you when you're cooking

To make your macaroons:

Preheat the oven to 170°C/325°F/Gas 3.

1. Beat the egg whites until they form soft peaks.
   Add the sugar gradually and continue whisking
   until the peaks are firm and shiny.
2. Carefully fold in the coconut, vanilla extract
   and salt.
3. Use an ice-cream scoop to form the macaroons
   and place each one on the lined baking sheet.
4. Bake for 15 minutes and then transfer to a
   wire rack to cool.

To decorate:

1. Melt the chocolate by breaking it into squares and placing it in a heatproof bowl set over a pan of boiling water. You can also do this in the microwave by heating the chocolate for around a minute. Stir it to get rid of any lumps.

2. Pour the hundreds and thousands into a small bowl.

3. To transform your macaroons into sea urchins, dip each macaroon first into the bowl of melted chocolate and then into the hundreds and thousands.

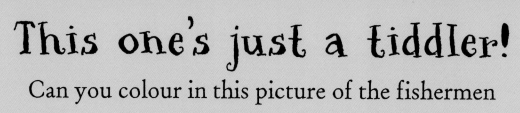

This one's just a tiddler!

Can you colour in this picture of the fishermen
throwing Tiddler back to sea?

Dreaming Up a Story!

There are lots of fish in the sticker section at the back
of the book. Can you find them and put them in the ocean?

Bobbing Along!

Who's this swimming along the ocean floor?
Join the dots to find out.

The Story-Telling Fish

Can you colour in this picture of Tiddler?

Wibble, Wobble!

Make a beautiful jellyfish to hang in your room!

1. Paint the outside of one of the paper bowls in whatever colour you like. This will turn into the body of your jellyfish.

2. Cut out a pair of circles from the white card and colour in two black dots to make eyes.

3. When the painted bowl is dry, you can decorate it with different-coloured designs: circles, stripes or even some zigzags!

4. Stick the eyes to the front of the painted bowl.

5. Turn the second bowl upside-down and stick some ribbons around the edge with tape.

6. Stick some more ribbons underneath the second bowl, so that your jellyfish has lots of tentacles.

7. Now cover the outside of the unpainted bowl with glue and stick it inside the painted bowl, making sure that the ribbons dangle down.

8. Once the glue has dried, pierce a hole through the top of the bowls and thread some string or a ribbon through.

9. Knot the string on the underside so that you can hang your jellyfish up!

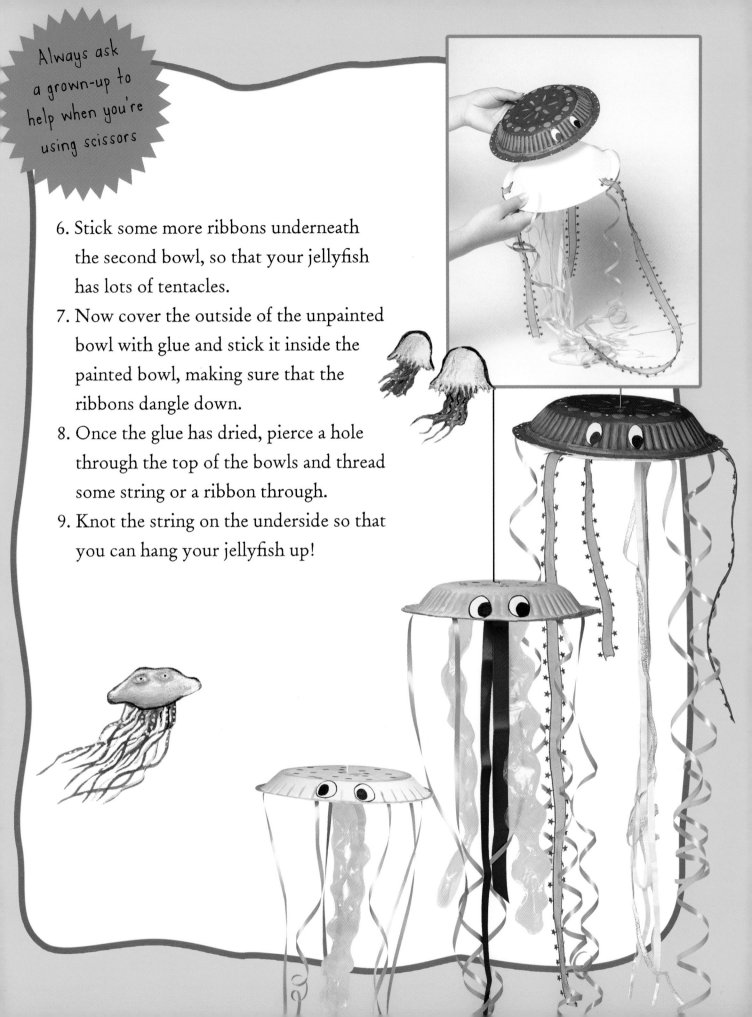

Fish Mosaic

Find the brightly coloured scales in the
sticker section at the back of the book.
Use these to make your fish shimmer!

These are the stickers for the "Fishermen" Jigsaw.

These are the stickers for your Fish Mosaic.

These are the stickers for the "Shipwreck" Jigsaw.